Thinking About SEO in Financial Services and Fintech

Roggie Clark

Learn More SEO From Me

Below, I included links to several SEO books I've written. They are excellent reads.

The ABCs of SEO: Search Engine Optimization 101

https://www.amazon.com/ABCs-Search-Engine-Optimization-Page-ebook/dp/B0C2JSLW7M

The Technical SEO Handbook

https://www.amazon.com/Technical-SEO-Handbook-Learn-Issues-ebook/dp/B0CMBJR9QV

The SEO and Web Developer Collaboration Guide

https://www.amazon.com/SEO-Web-Developer-Collaboration-Guide-ebook/dp/B0DHLBM48C

Learn HTML and Javascript From Me

The Basics of JavaScript Coding For Beginners: Learn Basic JavaScript Programming Concepts in less than 50 pages

https://www.amazon.com/Basics-JavaScript-Coding-Beginners-Programming-ebook

The Basics of HTML (Hypertext Markup Language) Coding For Beginners: Learn Foundational HTML Programming Concepts

https://www.amazon.com/Basics-Hypertext-Markup-Language-Beginners-ebook

Learn How To Invest in Silver With This Book

Whether you're approaching retirement or already enjoying it, protecting and growing your wealth is critical. This book is your clear, no-nonsense guide to incorporating silver into your wealth-building strategy.

https://www.amazon.com/Stacking-Silver-Budget-Beginners-Strategies-ebook/dp/B0FQPS6NT3

Learn Macro and Micro Economics, With This One Book

Whether you're a student, a professional, or simply someone eager to understand the world around you, this book is your perfect introduction to the fundamentals of micro and macroeconomics.

https://www.amazon.com/Macro-Micro-Economics-Workbook-Beginners-ebook/dp/B0FVHGVTFB

Copyright

Title: Thinking About SEO in Financial Services and Fintech
Author: Roggie Clark

Cover Design: Roggie Clark
Editing: Renee' Clark

Printed in the United States of America

Disclaimer

The views and opinions expressed in this book are those of the author and do not necessarily reflect the official policy or position of any individual, company, or organization cited or referenced in the text.

The author is not affiliated with any of the individuals, companies, or organizations mentioned in the text, nor does the author receive any form of compensation for citing or referencing them. Some sample scenarios in this text are fictitious. Any similarity to actual persons, living or dead, is purely coincidental.

The professional information (strategies, tips, and concepts) in this text is provided on an "as is" basis, without warranties of any kind, express or implied. While every effort has been made to ensure the accuracy of the information contained herein, neither the author nor the publisher makes any representations or warranties regarding its completeness, reliability, or applicability. The information is for educational and informational purposes only and should not be interpreted as professional, legal, financial, or business advice.

This book does **not** constitute financial advice, investment guidance, or legal counsel. Any financial, business, or investment decisions made based on this book are done **at your own risk**. You should always conduct your own research and consult a **certified financial**

advisor, legal professional, or other qualified expert before making any decisions that could impact your finances, business, or legal standing.

Neither the author nor the publisher guarantees any specific results or outcomes. By reading this book, you acknowledge and agree that the author and publisher shall not be held liable for any direct, indirect, incidental, or consequential damages, financial losses, or harm arising from the use or misuse of the information contained in this text. You assume full responsibility for any actions taken based on the content of this book.

Consulting, Coaching Services, Or Podcast Appearances

I know that from reading this book, it simply may not be enough information for you; you may require more personalized support with your unique business situation, or you want to share my thoughts along with your content. So, because of that, I'm offering the opportunity to receive consulting, coaching, and podcast appearances from me on SEO and AI. As far as coaching and consulting, I can offer support with:

- Creating SOPs (Standard Operating Procedures)
- Creating SEO strategies
- Content Suggestions
- Technical Audits
- Web design/migrations
- Competitor analysis
- Keyword research
- SEO Career Coaching

For podcasting, I can:

- Set up a paid podcast appearance or guest blog post with me, with a contract in writing, with dates, times, and resources that are needed from you.
- Help with the promotion of said podcast after I finish appearing in it.

- Provide discounted copies of any of my SEO or Web Developer books and negotiate a royalty payment split in exchange for acting as an affiliate for my books, courses, templates, etc.

If you are interested in any of these services or collaboration opportunities, and would like to request more information for a specific need you may have.

Please email me at **bouncerankseo@gmail.com**. In your email, please include the following information:

- Your name
- The business you represent (if applicable)
- Team size (if applicable)
- What service or collaboration opportunity do you want
- Any other important information I should know about you

My administrative assistant will email you back within 24 - 48 hours with rates and an information sheet for you to review. Thank you so much for your time and interest in working with me!

Table of Contents

Introduction

Financial services and fintech all center around the same thing, and that is moving money, except with fintech, you might get a shoddy, lackluster app to go with it. In this space, everything here is amplified: **trust matters more, scrutiny is higher, and every decision carries weight**. People don't casually scroll through financial products the way they do fashion, gadgets, or streaming apps. Money is personal. Money is serious. Every mistake is visible, and every misstep can stick.

Also, people are relentlessly honest; you can't just pop up with a financial service tomorrow and think people aren't going to let you know how bad it sucks. This is people's money, livelihood, savings, retirement, whatever people did to get the money. When you offer financial services, you are basically becoming a **fiduciary** whether you want to or not. So trust is not key — it's the only thing that'll keep your lights on, unless you can subsidize it and mimic trust by censoring complaints, but again — that's not going to last long. Shadow banking is already facing heavy scrutiny and regulation on a daily basis – so anything you can do to keep your fintech out of the eyes of consumer protection agencies and watchdog groups is not just important — it's the only way to truly maintain successful business operations long-term.

This book isn't a guide. It isn't a how-to. I'm not here to tell you what works, what doesn't, or how to "optimize" anything. Most of that guidance out there is garbage anyway. The advice that claims to teach you "SEO for fintech" usually misses the point: this space isn't about tactics, it's about reality and transparency.

There is no amount of AI, no algorithmic magic, that can overcome the fundamental fact that fintech is a heavily watched space with a specific set of rules that must be followed in order to avoid stricter regulation. SEO, and all the "fun" tactics that so many "pros" swear by, should be so stripped down in this space that it honestly shouldn't be called SEO at all. Essentially, what I am saying is it all just culminates to maintaining basic website etiquette — if you want to call it SEO, sure, but that's all it is, making sure your website exudes trust, reliability, and credibility. In other words, the strategies are more about simple technical applications, public relations, and basic common sense than any quack on an SEO blog can tell you.

I think that's why so many SEOs fail in this space, or get it kinda right, because they think they can try all the typical SEO magic in this space, but get humbled real quick when they see how low the conversion rates are. Yeah, they get traffic, and even clicks, but in finance and fintech, that means nothing — people want conversions. So again, what this book is is a look from the inside. Observations from someone who's been in the trenches, seen the patterns, and watched the hype and the failures play out. It's about credibility, visibility, and how the audience actually behaves when money is involved.

You won't find step-by-step instructions here. You won't find checklists or formulas. You will find the unvarnished truth about the environment, the quirks, the tensions, and the patterns that anyone paying attention can see. Take it or leave it. That's the point. This isn't about helping anyone win at SEO or holding your hand. It's about showing what the space actually looks like, unfiltered, uncensored, and stripped of all the nonsense that passes for expertise these days. So if you want to go to your nearest search engine, and keyword search "SEO for fintech" and read the crappy blogs on the results page, be my guess, but think to yourself — if that crap actually worked, then why is the financial industry in shambles, and suffering from record debt, no trust, and a huge number of failures?

I am hoping that if you picked this book up, you already looked at that stuff, and tried it already, and realized it didn't work, and that whatever "results' you think it is producing is just vanity — but if not, just go back and do that, because this book might not be for you. Nonetheless, let's get into Chapter 1.

Chapter 1: The Digital Finance Shift and Thinking About Strategy

In this chapter, I want to talk about how to set up your basic SEO strategy, like how to pick your main keyword, but before I do that, I have to talk to you about fintech and how the landscape creates a unique perspective for setting up an actual SEO strategy. Let's keep it real, the financial world used to be a place of brick-and-mortar banks, branch managers, and forms you had to sign in triplicate. People trusted the institutions because they had no other choice, and the system moved at its own pace. Transparency was rare, and the concept of a "black box" was in full effect.

Then came fintech. Apps, online accounts, instant transfers, payment processors, robo-advisors. Suddenly, the rules changed. Consumers didn't just want convenience — they wanted control, speed, and transparency. Banks that had relied on legacy systems found themselves playing catch-up, and startups appeared to leapfrog decades of tradition in months. Visibility became a different game. It wasn't about being the biggest name in town anymore, or buying out all the competitors — it was about being the brand that felt credible, reliable, and trustworthy online. The platforms, interfaces, and messages mattered as much as the products themselves.

The shift also changed expectations. Customers began to assume that everything would be instant, secure, and frictionless. Any hiccup could damage your reputation faster than ever before. The digital space exposed weaknesses and amplified mistakes. In short, the financial industry moved from a slow, controlled environment to a fast, transparent one, where perception and credibility carry as much weight as just offering the products and services. In other words you just offering consumers access to financial services (cheap credit, payment processors, P2P lending, etc.) is not enough to gain long-term users — the app, and overall customer experience have to actually be good. So this essentially takes lobbying out of the equation and returns power back to the consumer. So, understanding this shift isn't about tactics. It's about recognizing the reality: the game changed, and what matters now is your actual reputation, and not just your ability to exist.

So, how does that tie into SEO? Well, simply it means that just showing up at the top of a search engine is moot – being at the top is not going to stop people from going through your website with a fine-tooth comb if they are actually serious about utilizing your financial products. In financial services, traffic is not important; one lead, potential client, or user can very well keep a department running for months, what matters is quality, and to get quality leads, you must build genuine authority, build genuine trust, and maintain a consistent, reliable experience – in SEO terms this means adhering to typical On-Page SEO, Technical SEO, and Link-Building strategies that all the fake gurus swear by — but I want to make this clear, other than just using those terms — that's all the "SEO" that's really in there, I kind of talked about that a bit in the introduction — when I get into the next chapter, I'll explain what I really mean, but for now just know that I am talking about stepping out of the typical computerize SEO framework, and getting back to basic human interaction — that's what keeps financial services moving — one real review from an SEO lead is going to keep your fintech operating longer than any chart claiming to show you all the "keywords" you rank for — what difference does it make ranking for keywords if no one converts from them?

So right now, just get that out of your head, any of that SEO mumbo jumbo — when it comes to just getting the strategy right, you just need to be clear about what your main offering, and possible supplemental offerings are, and what words they would use to find them. So if you offer peer-to-peer lending, that's your main keyword; if you offer payment processing — that's your main keyword, now's not the time to be fancy – if you can't describe what the hell you offer in one or two words, don't expect anyone else to.

So forget about the whatever keyword tool you are about to use, and just put your thinking cap on and get clear about what your main offering or keyword is, because once you have that, everything else is simple. Because when people look up your company, they are going to use this main offering as the keyword, and definitely your brand name, so again, trust is important — in the next chapter, let's talk a bit more about trust and how to build it.

Chapter 2: The Trust Factor

In finance, trust isn't just important — it's everything. Unlike other industries, where a flashy ad or a clever campaign can sway someone, financial services live and die by credibility. People don't hand over their money lightly, and they certainly don't forgive mistakes easily.

Trust shows up in subtle ways. It's in the clarity of communication, the transparency of fees and terms and conditions, the reputation and reviews of the company, and the way problems are handled when they arise. It's why most brands seem solid on the search engine results page, but when you click into their website instantly, the experience falls short — it feels sketchy the moment you start digging. The rise of digital finance hasn't made trust easier. If anything, it has made it harder. Everything is visible online — reviews, complaints, praise, missteps. One slip, one miscommunication, and the ripple effect can be huge. The challenge isn't just being competent; it's being perceived as competent, ethical, and reliable, all at the same time.

This is why credibility in financial services often outweighs almost everything else. Products, pricing, and features matter, but not as much as the sense that a company is legitimate, careful, and aligned with the customer's interests. In fintech, this tension is even more pronounced. Startups can move fast and innovate, but speed comes with scrutiny. Legacy institutions may move slowly, but they carry the weight of long-standing reputation, which, from what I have observed in the financial industry, is often poor. In every case, trust is the invisible currency — more valuable than any marketing spend, more fragile than any product feature.

So with that said, when it comes to content and on-page SEO, it is not about "ramping up", or flooding the zone with as many AI articles as you can write — honestly it's about cleaning up your branded content – like your hompage, service pages, pricing page, and customer service pages, so that they are clean, transparent, and get people the information they need quickly, because again, like I said in the last chapter people are mainly going to use your company name to find you — also, FAQs (frequently asked questions) are going to matter a lot more because people already feel a slight sense of worry, so anything you can do on the page to alleviate that worry will be helpful.

This is why I say something as simple as making a dedicated page to your customer service line is important — and let me just go ahead and be clear about this — if you don't want it to be easy for customers to get in touch with you or find you because you are running some type of scam — just go ahead and forget it because that's not what this is about.

The goal is authenticity, for instance, for a lender — one clear page that addresses each unique lending situation, and what the actual terms are — no matter how high the interest rate you want to charge — is going to get you further than if you omit that information. In fintech SEO, transparency is key — so you should never complain about not having content ideas because your next content idea could just be you going back to your main pages and making them clearer and transparent. Last thing I'll share when it comes to finance on-page SEO, is less text is more — SEOs love to fill pages with walls of text — so do many financing institutions, but people actually want short, quick, spaced out text that get's them what they need quickly — again when it comes to finance, legal, insurance, or anything that is stressful for people, something as simple as you having blocked text, in a small font could be the difference between people feeling confident and reaching out to you, and them feeling overwhelmed and not reaching out.

So again, sometimes your "on-page SEO" or content brief might just be you making your pages look less overwhelming and more inviting. So, to close, again, it's all about transparency and accountability.

Chapter 3: Authority Without Risk

In financial services, authority isn't just earned — it's carefully maintained. Every claim, every statement, every public-facing message is scrutinized. Misstep even once, and credibility takes a hit that can linger far longer than anyone expects. Brands in this space walk a fine line. They need to appear knowledgeable, confident, and innovative, but without ever stepping into territory that feels risky, misleading, or untrustworthy. That tension defines how visibility is built and maintained. The loudest voices aren't always the most trusted — subtle, consistent signals of reliability often carry more weight than marketing noise.

Startups and newer fintech companies face a unique challenge. They want to make an impression, push boundaries, and grow fast. But growth can't come at the expense of credibility, and a possible cease and desist letter. Traditional institutions, on the other hand, rely on legacy reputation, often moving slowly, but are more easily protected from scrutiny due to their long-standing connections. Both approaches reveal a simple truth: in finance, authority is fragile, and it's closely tied to the perception of caution and competence. That's not something you can just censor and ignore — like risk in finance, reputation is like a boomerang, the same complaint that you ignore today on a review page, could very well be the one that leads to a lawsuit and poor press tomorrow.

It's also clear that authority is more about perception than reality. A fintech may be genuinely capable, but if that competence isn't visible or recognized, it doesn't matter. Conversely, small signals of diligence — clear communication, thoughtful design, transparency — can reinforce credibility far more effectively than overt self-promotion. In this world, visibility and authority must coexist with caution. The more public the presence, the more potential risk. Every step forward is measured, even if it looks effortless from the outside.

So what I am basically saying is, that when it comes to doing Off-Page SEO in this space — it's not worth it to play the link-building game — instead you should be focused on creating genuine partnerships with your users — without a doubt, most of if not all of them are business owners, and have websites — so on a more SEO level, you creating some widget that can live on their website that links up your financial app, is going to translate to real authority building, more than flooding the zone with a bunch of fake backlinks. Also, you taking the time to interview and talk to real users and share their stories on your website is going to build you more authority than some hapless case study. Basically, what I am saying is the typical public relations game of showing up on Forbes or CNBC ain't gonna cut it — these sites don't have the credibility or weight they once had so instead of trying to chase vanity — focus more on working with your users — it could be as simple as offering some perk in exchange for a review or interview with your fintech that you can promote on your blog — that is going to go over better with users.

I also want to mention this is not about "virtue signaling" if you don't really care about your users, doing this stuff is just going to come across as shallow and disingenuous. Lastly, to talk about reviews, again, contrary to typical SEO strategy, your "link building strategy" should be more focused on "social proof engineering" and thinking of ways to get genuine reviews from real customers — this proof, again, is going to weigh more heavily than just showing up at the top of Google.

So this is the time to respond to reviews — even if they are bad, or are saying something you don't like, because people see how you handle disputes and weigh that heavily in their decision-making process.

Chapter 4: Understanding Financial Audiences and Reliability Building

People act differently when money is involved. In almost every other market, impulse, curiosity, or entertainment can drive behavior. In financial services, caution dominates. Every decision is weighed, every option scrutinized, and every risk considered. Something as simple as a slightly slow website can instantly deteriorate trust — why, because people don't play about their money or time, so when it comes to financial services, they expect perfection and nothing less.

The audience isn't homogeneous. Some are tech-savvy early adopters, comfortable with apps and digital wallets. Others are conservative, slow to change, and skeptical of anything new, and need a screen reader. What unites them all is a need for assurance — reassurance that their money is safe, that they're making the right choice, and that the company they're dealing with is competent and credible. Understanding this audience isn't about segmentation charts or personas. It's about recognizing the mindset: cautious, deliberate, and deeply aware of stakes. They may never tell you what they're thinking, but their choices speak volumes. And for anyone observing the space, those choices reveal patterns that are hard to ignore.

With that being said, when it comes to doing technical SEO in this space, you shouldn't be thinking about filling your website with bells and whistles – a simple theme, minimal design, and clean code are all you need to be successful — in this space, less is not just more — it's the rule of the land. Also, like I was saying earlier, speed and performance are the only thing that matters, so if you are a fintech company, and I can't believe I have to say this, but you shouldn't be being cheap on your website hosting and performance. Get good hosting, and avoid any WYSIWYG (what you see is what you get) content management system like Wix, Squarespace, Shopify, or anything like that — this not a WordPress plug, but until I find something that can outperform these other CMSs — I always recommend this to my client as a good way to get a balance of customization, with simplicity.

Also, again, it's the little things that count — so you taking the time to make sure that proper alt text is included on your images, that proper captions are included on your videos, and that proper descriptions are included on your blog posts is important — all of these things add up and make a big difference in terms of accessibility, which goes hand and hand with technical SEO.

Last thing I'll share is basically ignore anything about schema markup or anything super technical you hear from an SEO blog or some pseudo expert — it's all hearsay, and 99% of it is just correlational, but not actually causational — technical SEO in fintech is just about having a fast, reliable website, that takes people from point A to B quickly and simply, so spend more time getting your site's taxonomoy, and prevent broken links, than trying to outsmart search engines, and users.

Conclusion

Financial services and fintech are complicated, high-stakes, and constantly shifting. Visibility, credibility, and trust define success in ways that are obvious yet often ignored. The patterns are there for anyone paying attention: the cautious audience, the fragile authority, the tension between speed and regulation.

This book isn't a guide. It doesn't tell you what to do or how to do it. It's a reflection of reality, a lens into the world of financial SEO and digital finance as it exists today. I did my best to share, for lack of better words, "tactics" in each of the SEO domains (on-page, off-page, and technical) that I have actually used. Take the observations, the nuances, and the insights as you will — or leave them because chances are, if you know anything about finance, then you would know that past results do not guarantee future performance — so your goal should be to look at these things as a guide for how you should move forward. There's no step-by-step formula, no magic shortcut — you have to do the work.

The real story of financial services shouldn't be about tactics or tricks. It should be about understanding the environment, respecting the stakes, and seeing the space for what it is: complex, unforgiving, and fascinating. Success here shouldn't be earned overnight, and it shouldn't be guaranteed by any checklist. It should come from navigating the realities, acknowledging the patterns, and recognizing the human factors that no algorithm or guidebook can replace.

At the end of the day, the lesson — if there is one — is simple: visibility, credibility, and trust aren't optional in finance. They're the fundamentals, whether anyone bothers to talk about them or not. So again, if you are serious about improving your SEO, it is hyper critical that you basically ignore all the SEO advice you see, and instead just focus on creating the most valuable, trustworthy and credible brand you can — if you do it's a side effect that users will start looking your services up more, and obviously it's going to translate to a potentially bigger SEO traffic and thus more traffic. Take care.

About the Author

Roggie "Raj" Clark is an entrepreneur and a 10-year marketing professional with a proven track record in e-commerce and digital business growth. Having built and managed successful online stores with thousands of sales and consulted for numerous marketing clients, Roggie has mastered the intricacies of online marketing, branding, and consumer behavior. He has also written several popular books on digital marketing, SEO (search engine optimization), and programming (HTML, CSS, and JavaScript).

As a former marketing manager at a fintech company—a role he secured through his own marketing and financial expertise—Roggie gained firsthand experience in financial strategy and wealth-building.

www.ingramcontent.com/pod-product-compliance
Lightning Source LLC
LaVergne TN
LVHW022327200926
848481LV00004B/1450
9798295567988